D1116055

Life Under the Sea

Whales

by Cari Meister

Bullfrog Books

Ideas for Parents and Teachers

Bullfrog Books give children practice reading informational texts at the earliest reading levels. Repetition, familiar words, and photo labels support early readers.

Before Reading

- Discuss the cover photo. What does it tell them?
- Look at the picture glossary together. Read and discuss the words.

Read the Book

- "Walk" through the book and look at the photos. Let the child ask questions.
- Read the book to the child, or have him or her read independently.

After Reading

- Prompt the child to think more. Ask: What things are different among the whales shown in this book?

Bullfrog Books are published by Jump!
5357 Penn Avenue South
Minneapolis, MN 55419
www.jumplibrary.com

Library of Congress Cataloging-in-Publication Data
Meister, Cari.
  Whales / by Cari Meister.
    p. cm. -- (Bullfrog books: life under the sea)
  Summary: "This photo-illustrated nonfiction story for young readers describes how whales are mammals that need air and how different types of whales find food. Includes picture glossary"--Provided by publisher.
  Includes bibliographical references and index.
  ISBN 978-1-62031-009-0 (hdb. : alk. paper)
  1. Whales--Juvenile literature. I. Title.
QL737.C4M43 2013
599.5--dc23
                                    2012008436

Series Editor: Rebecca Glaser
Series Designer: Ellen Huber
Production: Chelsey Luther & Heather Dreisbach

Photo Credits: Alamy, 13; Dreamstime, 3, 9, 22, 23tl; iStockphoto, 6-7, 23tr; National Geographic Stock, 15, 21, 23bl; Shutterstock, 1, 4, 8, 12, 16, 22, 24; Superstock, cover, 5, 10-11, 14-15, 16-17, 18-19, 19, 23br

Printed in the United States of America at Corporate Graphics in North Mankato, Minnesota
7-2012/ PO 1125
10 9 8 7 6 5 4 3 2 1

Table of Contents

Whales Under the Sea

A big blue whale swims.
She's the biggest
animal in the world.

Whales live in the ocean.
But they are not fish.
They are mammals.
They need air.

A blowhole is like a nostril. It lets old air out.

blowhole

It takes fresh air in.

Look! There she blows!

Her spout is big.

Now she dives.
She pumps her
tail to go fast.

flipper

Her flippers help steer.

13

She is hungry!
She sees a school
of krill.
Yum!

krill

squid

Not all whales eat krill.
Sperm whales have teeth.
They eat squid.

Humpback whales work together to get food.

They blow bubbles.

The bubbles make nets.

The nets catch cod.

Now it's time to play!

Parts of a Whale

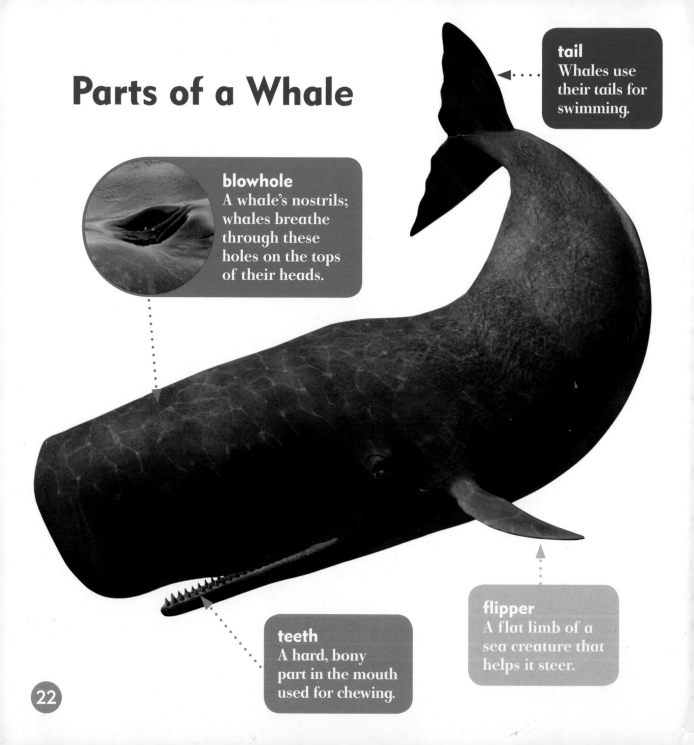

tail
Whales use their tails for swimming.

blowhole
A whale's nostrils; whales breathe through these holes on the tops of their heads.

teeth
A hard, bony part in the mouth used for chewing.

flipper
A flat limb of a sea creature that helps it steer.

Picture Glossary

cod
A kind of fish from the Atlantic Ocean.

mammal
A warm-blooded animal that makes milk for its young.

krill
A small, shrimp-like fish eaten by whales.

spout
A jet of water that a whale blows from its blowhole.

Index

To Learn More

Learning more is as easy as 1, 2, 3.

1) Go to www.factsurfer.com

2) Enter "whale" into the search box.

3) Click the "Surf" button to see a list of websites.

With factsurfer.com, finding more information is just a click away.

24